KIDDING AROUND

Philadelphia

A YOUNG PERSON'S GUIDE TO THE CITY

REBECCA CLAY

ILLUSTRATED BY KIM WILSON EVERSZ

THIRD GRADE READING

John Muir Publications
Santa Fe, New Mexico

for my mother and father, Cathy and Fred.
for my daughter, Jennifer.
for Jeffrey Cohen and Linda May, and
for the City of Brotherly Love.
My thanks to one and all!

John Muir Publications, P.O. Box 613, Santa Fe, NM 87504

First edition. First printing

Library of Congress Cataloging-in-Publication Data

Clay, Rebecca, 1956-
  Kidding around Philadelphia : a young person's guide to
the city / Rebecca Clay : illustrated by Kim Wilson
Eversz. — 1st ed.
     p. cm.
  Summary: A travel guide to the city with information
about its history, culture, and people.
  ISBN 0-945465-71-8
  1. Philadelphia (Pa.)—Description—1981- —Guide-
books—Juvenile literature. 2. Children—Travel—
Pennsylvania—Philadelphia—Guide-books—Juvenile
literature. [1. Philadelphia (Pa.)—Description—Guides.]
I. Eversz, Kim Wilson, ill. II. Title.
F158.18.C57   1990
917.48'110443—dc20   90-6406
                                                          CIP
                                                           AC

Typeface: Trump Medieval
Designer: Joanna V. Hill
Typesetter: Copygraphics, Santa Fe, N.M.
Printer: Guynes Printing Company of New Mexico
Printed in the United States of America

Distributed to the book trade by:
W. W. Norton & Company, Inc.
New York, New York

Contents

1. City of Brotherly Love

Robert Indiana created the LOVE sculpture to celebrate America's bicentennial in 1976. You can see it across the street from City Hall.

That's exactly what Philadelphia means in Greek—the City of Brotherly Love. William Penn gave Philadelphia its name way back in 1682 when he founded it where the Delaware River meets the Schuylkill. Then, the marshy area was inhabited by a few Swedish settlers and Indian tribes.

Little did Mr. Penn know that his tiny Quaker settlement would turn into the most exciting center of the New World's revolution against England. Or that Philadelphia would be the capital of a brand-new nation from 1790 to 1800.

He probably never thought Philadelphia would grow to be the second-largest city in the Northeast, either, or the fifth largest in the country by the 1990s. But remember, Philadelphia is not the capital of Pennsylvania. The state's center of government is Harrisburg.

On this trip, you'll crisscross the city, going back and forth in time. From block to block, you'll travel across the centuries; from the eighteenth-century colonial period, when men in velvet and lace created a new concept in government, to the late twentieth century, when men and women in business suits zoom in eleva-

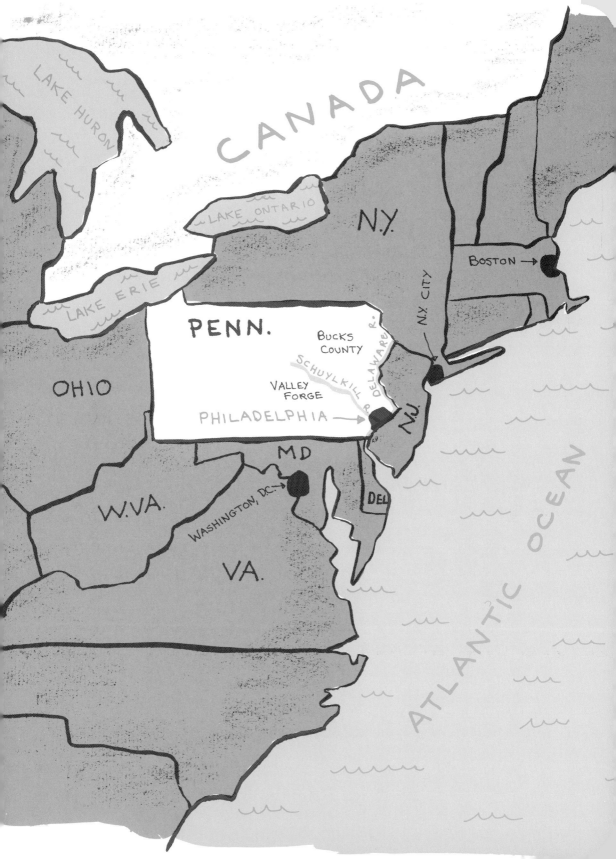

tors to their offices high up in glassy skyscrapers.

Probably the best person to give you a tour of Philadelphia would have been Ben Franklin himself. After all, he's responsible for a lot of its basic services and character. After you've been in Philadelphia for a while, you'll think he must have built the whole place himself, too.

And let's not forget George Washington, John Adams, or Thomas Jefferson. It was right here in Philadelphia that the Declaration of Independence and the Constitution of the United States were written and signed. It's hard to imagine how different America would be without those famous men and their documents.

You'll actually touch the great symbol of our country's freedom, the Liberty Bell. People say stroking its bronze curves will give you good luck.

And when you walk east toward the Delaware River and its freshwater port, you'll climb aboard a famous battleship and squeeze yourself through a submarine.

You'll also visit some of the greatest museums in the United States. The science museums will keep you busy for hours with hands-on exhibits

In 1670, at the age of 26, William Penn received 26 million acres of land in the New World from King Charles II. He called it Pennsylvania.

6

and a realistic trip to the stars. A life-size dino-saur will speak to you, directly, and you can sit in the cockpit of a World War I fighter plane.

Recognize the broad stone steps that lead up to the Museum of Art? You're right. Those are the same ones that Sylvester Stallone ran up at the end of *Rocky I* and *Rocky II*. There used to be a statue of Sly as Rocky at the top of the steps, but the city decided to move it to the Spectrum, where most of Philadelphia's big sports events take place.

And then you'll visit America's very first zoo, the Philadelphia Zoo. Ride a pony, make like a honeybee, and hang out with a chimp.

Plus, Philadelphia is the only city in the whole world where you'll see the mummers. Find out who they are!

The southernmost part of the original city used to end at South Street, which is still one of the most fun avenues in all of Philadelphia. In fact, some people say it was Martha Washing-ton's favorite place to go shopping way back in the 1700s.

This is just a tiny part of what the City of Brotherly Love has to show you. This guidebook is written especially for you, to help you enjoy all the attractions that Philadelphia is so proud of. And while you're visiting this great city, think about how Philadelphia and the country still struggle with the early principles that were envisioned right here.

When Penn and his Quaker followers arrived in their new colony, it was already inhabited by a few small settlements of Swedes and Dutch. There were also a number of Indian tribes who had been living in the area for over 12,000 years.

Today, 1.64 million people call Philadelphia their home.

2. Getting Around: The Basics

The best place to start your visit to Philadelphia is right at the **Independence National Historical Park Visitor Center**, on 3rd Street between Chestnut and Walnut streets. The National Park Rangers who run it are very friendly. No question is too silly, so ask them anything about where you want to go and what you want to see.

They'll also give you a free map of the historic district and some discount passes to the museums. With the passes, you could save enough for a snack. The center's gift shop has some neat items, including a copy of Thomas Jefferson's rough draft of the Declaration of Independence, in its original script. Or take home a mini Liberty Bell.

The center's film, *Independence*, is a good, easy way to catch up on your American history and get you primed for your tour. Remember, you're going to be exploring how this country was born.

You can do that on foot, on the subway, on a city bus, on a special trolley tour, or start out with a quick carriage ride around the historic neighborhood.

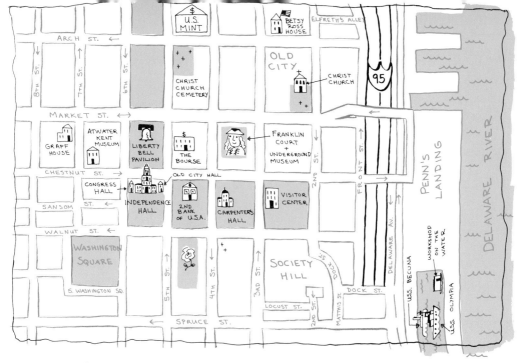

You might want to take a trolley tour first and then go back on foot to see those places that interested you the most. One suggestion is the **American Trolley Tours**. They pick up passengers at most of the big hotels for a morning tour and an afternoon tour. Plus there are plenty of taxis crisscrossing the city all day and all night long.

For information on sights and events in the rest of the city, drop by the **Visitors Center** at 1525 JFK Boulevard, across from City Hall. They'll have piles of material on all the regular and special events in town. Also, pick up the daily newspaper, *The Philadelphia Inquirer*, for its Weekend edition and an up-to-the-minute listing of movies, theater, music, and everything else.

It's best to avoid the subway if you can. And definitely never take it by yourself. There are plenty of city buses, but it's not always easy to

know which one to take. Check the maps at the bus stops and ask a bus driver which one to take for your destination. You can also ride an antique city trolley up 5th Street, down 4th Street, up 11th Street, or down 12th. It'll let you on and off at each intersection.

Or hop into a shiny horse-drawn carriage in front of Independence Hall. Listen to the horses' hooves clip-clop on the old cobblestone streets. Close your eyes and imagine you're somewhere back in the past.

Penn designed Philadelphia's Center City to work on a grid pattern where streets ran parallel and perpendicular to each other. That plan would keep all the traffic neat and orderly. He named the east/west streets after the trees growing in the area. The north/south streets are numbered beginning with Front Street at the Delaware River. The city started growing at the Delaware and spread west. That's why the most historic area is close to the docks on the Delaware.

7,000,000 people visit Independence National Historic Park every year.

11

3. Freedom!

Thomas Jefferson originally wrote a clause in the Declaration to ban slavery, but the delegation argued against it and it was dropped.

Imagine you are a boy or girl living in Philadelphia and it is the year 1776. You live in a British colony and you are a British subject. The king who rules you, your family, and your friends lives thousands of miles away, across a great ocean.

People in the other American colonies are taking up arms against the king, and you hear your parents arguing about independence with their neighbors. Many people think that the English taxes to import tea and cloth are very unfair. In Massachusetts, the colonists are saying, "No taxation without representation!" and are fighting for their rights.

Some people in Pennsylvania don't want to be free of England because they are still loyal to the Crown. But let's say you and your parents think it would be a great idea to get away from English rule and taxes. Let's say that you're patriots.

The first part of this step back into the past is the **Assembly Room** of **Independence Hall**, on Chestnut Street between 5th and 6th streets. The date is May 1776. The Second Continental Congress has been arguing and debating for days about how to free themselves of English

authority. Finally, they choose five men to write out a declaration. Thomas Jefferson, Benjamin Franklin, and John Adams are the most outspoken of those five.

Thomas Jefferson is chosen to do the actual writing because, as John Adams tells him, "You can write ten times better than I can." So Jefferson, who is a delegate from Virginia and only visiting Philadelphia at the time, heads over to the **Graff House** on the corner of Market and 7th streets. (The present house is mostly a reconstruction.) The Congress chose that rooming house for him to stay in because it was so quiet and away from city noise. Back then, it was a house in the country!

Jefferson stays there for eighteen days until he lays his quill pen down and the first draft of the Declaration of Independence is finished. It's now June 18, 1776. The Congress argues and debates some more over the wording, and finally, on the Fourth of July, the Congress accepts the Declaration.

On July 8, the big bronze **Liberty Bell** (Independence Mall, Market Street between 5th and 6th) rings out and thousands of people rush over

13

to find out what's going on. There is a man with a booming voice standing on a wooden platform reading the most famous words in American history.

"When in the course of human events. . ." he roars. "We hold these truths to be self-evident, that all men are created equal. That they are endowed by their creator with certain inalienable rights. That among these are life, liberty and the pursuit of happiness."

When he is finished, the crowd roars its approval. The Declaration is later written out on parchment. That's the copy that John Hancock and Jefferson, Franklin, Adams, and the other delegates sign in the Assembly Room. John Hancock signs his name especially big, just so that King George has no trouble reading it.

Then Ben Franklin makes a little joke that is funny in a way but maybe not so funny to these men who are putting their life on the line. He says, "Gentlemen, we must all hang together now, or we will hang separately." Remember, because they are colonists, they are now committing treason against the king, which is punishable by death!

Back to the present. When you're in the Assembly Room, there are some interesting things to look at. For example, the green linen-covered tables are copies because the originals were burned as firewood when the British got mad about all this independence stuff and occupied the city five months after the Declaration.

You must take a guided tour, which usually leaves every 15 minutes. The guide will point out things like the inkstand the signers used,

Jefferson's cane, and one of Franklin's books. And don't miss the "Rising Sun Chair" where George Washington sat while he headed the convention that wrote the Constitution of the United States in 1787 in that very same Assembly Room.

In the **Liberty Bell Pavilion**, you will find the big bell itself. Its famous crack has two pins and a brace in it to protect the crack from getting wider. The bell weighs a good 280 pounds. A National Park Service Ranger is always standing by the bell to answer any question you have. Don't be shy, they love to talk!

The ranger will also tell you it's just fine to go ahead and touch it. (Some say it'll bring you good luck.) The ranger may also tell you that this bell is the third one to be made in the same foundry in London and shipped to America. When the first bell arrived, it was strung up in a tree. When the people tried to ring it, the bell immediately cracked.

So it was melted down and a second bell was made. But this one had a dull ring. No one liked listening to it. So they melted it down again. Then finally, the third one sounded just right. But, as we all know, it cracked, too.

The name "Liberty Bell" actually came from the slavery abolitionists right before the Civil War.

4. Pennies and Piggy Banks

L et's think about Ben Franklin for a minute. We usually picture him as a round man with a bald head but long hair, wearing spectacles, and walking with a cane. But what's more important is all the things this man did and invented. He was like ten people in one!

The first place to go to learn more about Ben Franklin and how he helped change the world is to **Franklin Court**, at 314-322 Market Street, an unusual museum right on the spot where Franklin once owned a house. In fact, you'll see a special frame that was put up outside Franklin Court to show you exactly where that house stood.

The museum will also show you a fun little film about Ben Franklin, his family, and his life throughout the day in its own movie theater. It will tell you about his son, who, unlike Franklin, defended the British before and during the revolution. Put your feet up and stay for the film.

Now, before or after the film, you'll want to look over the display of furniture and household items that Franklin either owned or invented, like the Franklin stove. A room full of mirrors and neon lights will also remind you of Frank-

Ben Franklin was the first governor of Philadelphia. He served from 1785 to 1788.

lin's roles as scientist, inventor, statesman, printer, philosopher, and so on.

But keep going! In the **Franklin Exchange**, you'll find a whole set of phones. Pick one up and listen to what Franklin's friends, descendants, and enemies thought of him. Not everyone liked Ben. Most people thought he was a genius, but Mark Twain will tell you he was just a busybody. Oh, well, you can't please everyone.

In the Franklin Exchange, you'll also peer down into a sunken square in the floor where costumed dolls will act out some of Franklin's great diplomatic accomplishments. And farther on is another set of phones where you can get an earful of Franklin's opinions on everything from women to education. He wasn't shy!

Just so we don't forget, here are a few things that Ben Franklin invented. They may not seem like a big deal to us now, but remember, they didn't exist at all before Franklin created them. For example, he figured out that lightning was electricity and invented the lightning rod, which would carry the dangerous electricity away from buildings. That saved a lot of churches and houses from burning down. And since he also started the first insurance company, his invention saved his own company a lot of money.

Ben Franklin also founded America's first fire fighting company in Philadelphia in 1736. It was called the Union Fire Company and Fireman's Hall and is now the place to follow that important history. Today, **Fireman's Hall** on 2nd and Quarry streets is the national firehouse and museum of Philadelphia.

The museum is very proud of the many items it has from fire fighting's courageous past.

There's an authentic 1815 hand pumper, hand-sewn leather buckets the early firemen used in brigades, and the crude hatchets they used to chop their way into burning houses.

By 1736, Franklin had already been publishing his *Poor Richard's Almanac* for four years. The almanac was very popular because it gave people the weather forecast. Plus it contained a lot of wise sayings that kept his fellow Philadelphians on their toes.

Franklin also designed America's first cartoon. He wanted to show what would happen if the thirteen colonies didn't cooperate with each other. Back then, each colony only wanted to take care of itself and let the others take care of their own business. His cartoon made people think seriously about their future as a union.

Then, in 1753, the king appointed Franklin the first postmaster general of the American colonies. Well, in no time at all, Franklin figured out how to cut the mailing time way down. Instead of six weeks for a letter to go from Boston to Philadelphia, it only took about ten days.

And speaking of the mail, let's visit the **B. Free Franklin Post Office** right next to Franklin Court. Send a postcard to a grandparent or a friend. Ask the postal clerk to hand stamp it for you. The stamp will say *B. Free Franklin* in his handwriting!

America's first penny was also named after Franklin. It appeared in 1787, shortly after the Revolutionary War. Because at that time the only coins were still English, French, Dutch, and Spanish, the new country needed its own.

The "Franklin Penny" was made in Philadelphia, at the brand-new U.S. Mint. On one side the penny had a chain with thirteen links, representing the thirteen united colonies. The other side showed the sun and one of Franklin's favorite sayings from *Poor Richard's Almanac*, "Mind your business!"

Today, you can visit the fourth **U.S. Mint** building (5th and Arch sts.), where 1,500,000 coins are made every hour! Go upstairs in the Mint building to watch from observation windows overhead. Follow the process from the left. You'll watch tons of glittering blank coins travel around on conveyor belts to get stamped on both sides. It's a pretty awesome sight.

Philadelphia schoolchildren donated 80,000 pennies to create **Franklin's Bust**, near the corner of 4th and Arch. Look up and see Ben's big friendly face looking down at you. You'll see it's made up of tiny round circles. Those are the pennies. The plaque there also reminds us of another saying from *Poor Richard's Almanac*, "A penny saved is a penny earned."

When Ben Franklin died in 1790, he was buried at **Christ Church Burial Ground** at 5th and Arch, just a block from the Penny Bust. Go on in and toss a penny onto his grave. Women who had just gotten married used to do it for good luck back in the old days. And there is no doubt that Ben Franklin was well loved; 20,000 people showed up for his funeral.

Christ Church itself, on 2nd Street a half block from Market, was the highest point in the New World for many years. Seven signers of the Declaration of Independence worshiped there, and each had a private pew for his family. Look for their names on plaques by the pews.

Every February, Philadelphia celebrates Ben

Franklin's birthday. If you happen to be there then, check out the local newspapers and the Visitors Center for the many special events.

A good way to see what Philadelphia was like from 1680 to the early part of this century is to visit the **Atwater Kent Museum**, 15 South 7th. Its founder loved to invent things. In fact, he created some of our early radios.

He also had a passion for collecting things, and this museum has about 40,000 objects he picked up during his lifetime. There are beautiful old dolls, sunbonnets, rocking horses, military uniforms, and a selection of piggy banks. And you probably won't overlook the grandfather clock. It plays a lively French tune every hour.

Philadelphia was the capital of the United States from 1790 to 1800.

5. Wedding Cakes and Cheese Steaks

The statue of William Penn, on top of City Hall, was carved by Alexander Milne Calder in the late 1800s. The fountain sculpture at Logan Circle was carved by his son, Alexander Sterling Calder. And the huge white mobile in the Museum of Art was created by the second Calder's son, Alexander Calder. Philadelphians call the three sculptures, ''the Father, Son, and the Holy Ghost''!

uring the nineteenth century, influenced by France and Queen Victoria's England, Philadelphia built many distinctive buildings. Probably the best example of late Victorian and French Renaissance style is the **City Hall**, built in 1901. Philadelphians say it looks like a giant wedding cake, with all its tiers and decoration. And it really is huge. Its first floor covers five acres.

Take the elevator up to the base of **William Penn's statue** and watch the city spread out below you. Look a mile to the east to the Delaware River and a mile to the west to the Schuylkill. This is the only public place to see the city from a bird's-eye view, so get there early for the elevator. It only carries eight people at a time!

Face the northeast and you'll be facing the same direction as Penn's statue. It was positioned to look toward the site where Penn signed an important treaty with the Indians. It used to be the tallest point in Philadelphia until One Liberty Place was built during the last decade.

When you're down on the street again, on the Market Street/15th Street side, look at the corner to the southwest of City Hall. No, your eyes aren't playing a trick on you. That really is a

huge **clothespin**. Sculptor Claes Oldenburg dreamed it up for the Bicentennial in 1976.

If you're wondering about all the different architectural styles in the city and in the world, take a tour of the **Masonic Temple**, just on the other side of City Hall. It has seven lodge halls that will amaze you with their fantastic details.

The Masons constructed and reconstructed the vast halls to represent Renaissance, Ionic, Oriental, Corinthian, Gothic, Egyptian, and Norman architecture. Many people think the Egyptian is the best!

Are you hungry yet? Two blocks east of the Masonic Temple, you'll find the **Reading Terminal Market** and its hundreds of food markets and restaurant counters. Hop on a stool and order fish and chips or a bowl of spaghetti or an egg roll or a burrito. The terminal is packed at lunchtime because the food has a reputation for being very fresh and delicious.

Or you can head down to **The Gallery** and its collection of underground restaurant counters. Try a Philadelphia cheese steak there. That's strips of steak fried on a grill and stacked on a bulky roll with slices of cheese melting on it. Take plenty of napkins!

Or try a hoagie, a big roll with cold cuts, lettuce, and tomato. Maybe you call it a submarine sandwich where you come from. Only the Philadelphians call it a hoagie. And if it's summer, try a flavored water ice.

Now, if you happen to be on your way over to the historic area and it's not time for lunch yet, wait until you get to **The Bourse**, right across from the Liberty Bell. The building was constructed over a hundred years ago. Today, it's got three floors of shops and restaurants that look onto an open skylit atrium.

Go directly to the third floor on the escalators. As you're floating up toward your lunch, you'll probably hear the soft strains of live music. Look back. A pianist and other musicians are serenading you from the first floor. Or you might even catch a juggler or a clown in action!

Depending on your taste and appetite, you may order pizza, hoagies, steak sandwiches, salads, or ethnic food. And be ready to wait. Philadelphians love to eat here, too.

Now that that's been taken care of, let's head over to the **Betsy Ross House**, on Arch Street between 2nd and 3rd, where you'll find out more about the woman who is believed to have sewn the first American flag. The house is tiny, and the rooms are set up with life-size dolls. There's the children's room, with its rope mattress and cradle, and the upholstery shop where children worked. (They didn't have laws to protect against child labor back then.)

Betsy Ross was a Quaker seamstress. She married three times and had seven daughters.

6. Wampum Belts and a Nude Descending a Staircase

There are lots of ways to learn about history. You can read about it, and you can get up close to the real things that people used in their daily life.

Take the **Historical Society of Pennsylvania** (1300 Locust Street), for example. This working museum has such a fascinating collection of authentic stuff from Philadelphia's early years that you'll feel like you really did take a step backward in time.

The society's new permanent exhibit is called "Finding Philadelphia's Past: Visions and Revisions," and they aren't kidding. One of the first things you'll see when you get inside is the wampum belt that the Lenni-Lenape Indians gave William Penn as a sign of their friendship.

You'll see a heavy helmet left behind by a Swedish infantryman in the early 1600s. And there's George Washington's own personal camp knife and fork. Plus you can't miss the beautiful presentation swords and scabbards inlaid with gold and silver from the Civil War. And there's a whole lot more.

To learn more about what you're looking at, pick up the earphones that are scattered throughout the exhibit and push the button.

Between 1820 and the Civil War, Philadelphia's population grew from 110,000 to 560,000. Many were immigrant workers— English Protestants, Irish and German Catholics, and black Americans from the South.

You'll hear some pretty remarkable stories, including a history of the Underground Railroad as told in part by the great-grandson of a slave who used it to escape to the North.

If your legs are starting to wear out, take a seat in the museum's trolley car theater and watch some fast-paced films on Philadelphia's early days. Press your option on the video monitor, sit back, and relax.

If you're planning to visit Philadelphia for more than a week, you might want to think about attending the Historical Society's **Summer History Camp**. They have three one-week sessions. Call the society for more details.

When you were looking down on the city from the top of City Hall, you probably noticed a big imposing building at the end of the Ben Franklin Parkway. That's the **Philadelphia Museum of Art**, 26th Street and Ben Franklin Parkway. It has some amazing collections of art and artifacts from around the world.

If the weather's nice, definitely walk from City Hall to the Museum of Art. It's the same route that Rocky made famous. Start at the **LOVE sculpture** diagonally across the street from City Hall and head toward the museum. You'll pass through **Logan Circle** where you can take a rest by the huge fountain with carved figures around it.

It can take a long time to see everything in the museum, so here are a few suggestions on the exhibits you might enjoy most. First of all, take a look at Marcel Duchamp's *Nude Descending a Staircase* on the first floor. In 1913, this painting started a revolution in the history of art. It's very famous.

In 1876, in celebration of the country's bicentennial, Philadelphia held the first world's fair. Ten million people came to see it.

Suffragists Elizabeth Cady Stanton and Susan B. Anthony wrote the "Woman's Declaration of Rights" after women were not allowed into some of the world's fair events. Because of rain, and a shortage of seats inside, only men were allowed entrance.

Then head for the second floor and the **Arms and Armor** exhibit. You'll see great examples of light and heavy armor that men and children wore during the Middle Ages. Kids started practicing the joust with armor at the age of seven. Too bad the museum doesn't have a dressing room so you can try some on.

The museum has also reconstructed some examples of buildings you would only find in other countries. The **Hindu Temple Hall** from South India is the only real temple of its kind found in an American museum. Walk in and get a feel for what it would be like to be a Hindu worshiping in India. Or walk through a **Japanese teahouse** where the ancient tea ceremony would still be performed.

The museum is also proud of its many paintings by the greatest masters in the history of art. If you're thinking of becoming an artist or if you just enjoy fine art, wander through any of the museum's rooms for a taste of the best.

Now, let's head back to Logan Circle and the **Franklin Institute Science Museum**, 20th Street and Ben Franklin Parkway. The institute is the very first hands-on science center in America, and it's packed with all sorts of gadgets and games to help you learn about the world of science and have a blast at the same time. There's enough to do for a very full day, so plan to stick around.

The museum's newest section is the **Futures Center** created to give you a good idea of what to expect in the twenty-first century. You'll visit a space station and find out about the energy sources and environmental changes that will affect you when you grow up. And check out the real bionic man in action!

Plus, you won't want to miss the **Omniverse Theater**. The screen is as tall as a four-story building. Hold onto your seat! This show will blast you off into space where you'll watch a star be born and a whole lot more.

One place in the museum where you'll also find the most kids at one time is in the gigantic **walk-through heart**. The passageway leads to the lungs and back. Listen to the heartbeat and explanations while you're passing through.

You've seen your own shadow plenty of times, right? Well, have you ever seen it in color? Have you ever walked away from it while it stood still? Have you ever had it follow you in slow motion? Check it out!

Another popular room is the **Aviation Hall**, where you'll see an original Wright brothers Model B biplane and sit in the cockpit of a U.S. Air Force plane from World War I.

Fels Planetarium at the institute is a must. They have a brand new Digistar system that can re-create how the stars and planets looked at any date in history. When you look up at the enormous planetarium dome, you will really be amazed.

If you want to take some of these scientific adventures home with you, drop by the museum's gift shop. It's full of scientific objects and games to help you keep on learning.

Right behind the Franklin Institute Science Museum, you'll find the **Please Touch Museum**, 210 North 21st Street, for the younger kids. Do you have a little brother or sister who needs something quieter and smaller to do? The Please Touch Museum is the only museum in the country just for children seven years old and under. It will keep you both happy for a while. And it's full of make-believe.

First of all, there's often a mime or puppet show in the **Performance Center** on the first floor. Before you continue upstairs, find out if the museum has a special event scheduled.

How often do you really get to play dress-up? In this museum, you can put on the real suit of everyone from a fireman to a clown and see how bizarre you look in a distorted mirror.

There's the **Health Care Center** where you can play doctor or nurse and a real **TV mini-station** where you can anchor the Eyewitness News.

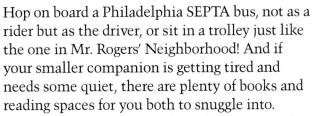

Hop on board a Philadelphia SEPTA bus, not as a rider but as the driver, or sit in a trolley just like the one in Mr. Rogers' Neighborhood! And if your smaller companion is getting tired and needs some quiet, there are plenty of books and reading spaces for you both to snuggle into.

If you like dinosaurs and all kinds of animals, head back to Logan Circle and the **Academy of Natural Sciences**, 19th Street and the Parkway. It's right next to the Franklin Institute on the circle, and it's been sharing the wonders of natural history since 1812. You can imagine our scientific knowledge has changed a lot since then.

The first rooms to check out are to the right of the information booth in the lobby. Turn around the corner and you'll be met by an enormous *Tyrannosaurus rex* skeleton with its jaws wide open. This hall is full of dinosaur bones and games to help you understand them.

Then walk through wide hallways on the second floor where a huge tiger is stalking its prey and Dall's sheep are tiptoeing up a steep mountainside. These are dioramas, where species from around the world are stuffed and put on display. And while you're thinking about how these animals exist in the wild, you'll hear a creature roaring somewhere off in the distance.

Follow that sound down to the first floor and you'll run into a full-size *Apatosaurus*. He'll move his head toward you and roll his eyes before he roars again. Don't be afraid. He's a mechanical cousin of the real thing. I think.

Finally, if you'd like to get your hands on something very real or very old, stop in at the **Outside-In** rooms on the third floor. You can see

some brightly colored African birds flitting around in a large cage and pick up a fat snake. There are also real fossils to touch and caves to crawl through.

Now, when you step out of the academy, you'll see two magnificent buildings across the circle. The one on the left is the **Free Library of Philadelphia**, Logan Circle, and it has Philadelphia's largest collection of children's literature. Do you love books old and new? This is definitely the spot for you.

If you're visiting the library on a weekday morning, take a tour of the Rare Book Department at 11:00. They'll show you things like a cuneiform tablet and a leaf from the Gutenberg Bible, the world's first printed book. Plus, there are always beautiful old illustrated children's books on display.

If you like the novels of Charles Dickens, ask
to see the original desk and candle the famous
English author used back in the nineteenth century. And if you're lucky, they'll show you Dickens's pet raven, Grip. He's stuffed but still kept in
a cage. When American writer Edgar Allan Poe
saw Grip for the first time, he got the idea to
write his very scary short story, "The Raven."

The Free Library also offers free films for
kids on Sunday afternoons. They start at 2:30,
and they're often packed, especially on a rainy
day. So get there early!

7. Mummers and Mummies

hen William Penn set up his colony of Pennsylvania, he asked that all residents respect the lifestyle and beliefs of their neighbors. Because of that ideal of tolerance, people from many different ethnic and religious groups settled in Philadelphia from all over the world. Today, the city and its suburbs are culturally diverse, although some groups have created neighborhoods with a distinctive identity.

They've also created museums to celebrate their own heritage and customs. One of the most outrageous events to take place in Philadelphia is the Mummer's Parade that marches up Broad Street every New Year's Day. And just to show off their fancy parade costumes and musical instruments all year 'round, the mummers have set up the **Mummer's Museum** at 2nd Street and Washington Avenue.

What is a mummer? An ordinary Philadelphia resident, adult and child, who would usually wear a suit and tie or jeans and a sweatshirt. Once a year, he or she puts on a fantastic costume that is bigger and more colorful than those in the Ice Capades. And each mummer dances the Mummer Strut to music you'd never hear anywhere else.

People in Philadelphia have been officially celebrating the Mummer's Parade since 1901, but its origins go way back to colonial America and to European and African cultural history. If you can't be in the city on New Year's Day, spend an hour at the Mummer's Museum. A videotape will teach you how to do the Strut, and you'll be amazed by the display of award-winning costumes.

The only museum in the entire country that's devoted to presenting exhibits on the role of Jews in the growth of the United States is right in Philadelphia, down by Independence Mall. It's the **National Museum of American Jewish History**, 55 North 5th Street. Its permanent exhibit, "The American Jewish Experience: From 1654 to the Present," is an exciting way to learn about the influence and impact of Jewish culture on our collective past.

While you're investigating the different religious and cultural influences on the character of Philadelphia and the nation, be sure to visit the **Afro-American Historical and Cultural Museum** at 7th and Arch streets. It's the very first museum built to display the history of black Americans in this country.

The museum building itself resembles African mud housing and starts you on your journey into the roots of black culture. Check out the **African Heritage Gallery** for exhibits and photographs on Afro-American styles and customs. Then move up to the second level for a powerful show on the history of slavery and captivity. You'll find out that there are places in the world where slavery still exists.

During the Civil War, Philadelphia was divided in its views toward slavery. Many factory owners relied on a steady supply of cotton from the south and were opposed to slave freedom. Other people simply did not want to see the Union dissolve and so fought to maintain it. But most Philadelphians condemned slavery on principle and helped run the Underground Railroad.

The upper three levels will remind you of the many contributions black Americans have made to the nation's history. Included are profiles of athletes, inventors, businessmen, jazz musicians, and the courageous men and women who fought in the civil rights movement.

Depending on your own ethnic roots and historical interests, you might want to stop by the **American Swedish Historical Museum**, 1900 Pattison Avenue. Remember, William Penn was not the first European to set foot on local soil. A tiny group of Swedes had been settled along the Delaware since before 1640, over thirty years before Penn arrived on the scene. In April, the museum presents Valborgsmassoafton, the Swedish community's spring festival, with folk dancing and Swedish treats.

In fact, the oldest part of Philadelphia is the part where the Swedes set up their little community. Today, it's called **Queen Village**, after the Swedish queen of the time, Christina. The borders of Queen Village are from Front to 6th streets and Lombard to Washington Avenue.

While you're thinking about all the different cultures that make up Philadelphia and America, consider visiting the **Balch Institute for Ethnic Studies**, 18 South 7th Street. It sounds a lot stuffier than it is. It's right next door to the place where Jefferson wrote the Declaration of Independence, so take a break to see how seriously our European, Oriental, and African ancestors took its message of freedom and equality. Check out the exhibit "Freedom's Doors: Immigrant Ports of Entry."

And one last very important place to explore other cultures is at the **University Museum of**

All over Philadelphia, you'll see vendors selling soft, warm pretzels. It's a local tradition to eat them with a fat squiggle of mustard on top.

America celebrated its 100th birthday at Fairmount Park with the Centennial Exposition. One hundred buildings were constructed for the event in 1876. Memorial House and Ohio House are the only two left.

Archaeology/Anthropology, 33rd and Spruce streets. It's the museum at the University of Pennsylvania, which, by the way, was also founded by Ben Franklin.

Do you like Egyptian mummies? This museum has a great show of mummies to share with you. There are also rooms full of fascinating things from other ancient and living civilizations, like Mesopotamia, China, and Alaska. If you're there on Saturday morning, and it's between October and March, stay for a special children's film at 10:30.

One ethnic neighborhood to be sure to visit is Philadelphia's **Chinatown**, with its beautiful Chinese Friendship Gate at the entrance. The Chinese have been living in this area for over 100 years. Chinese New Year is packed full of parades and other special events.

Plus, every day is crazy fun at the **Italian Market** on 9th Street between Christian and Federal. No supermarkets here. All the vendors have their products in open stalls and shops, just like in Europe. If you're lucky, you might even hear a butcher singing opera!

8. Down by the Rivers and on to the Zoo

efore you head over to the Delaware River docks, drop in at the **Philadelphia Maritime Museum**. If you love ships, you'll be in boat heaven when you see all the shipping gear this museum has on display. It also has every kind of model ship you can think of and a whole lot more.

Remember, during the 1700s and 1800s, Philadelphia was one of the top ports and ship-yards in the colonies and then in the country. Right before the American Revolution, about 880 ships docked along the sixty-six wharves that used to be there.

At the Maritime Museum, look at some of the gadgets that seamen used to hoist their huge sails and to navigate along the coast and across the oceans. Ask to see the museum's collection of real items from the giant cruise ship *Titanic* that sank in 1912. Plus, look over the model of the *Caledonia*. It was entirely carved out of bone, 120 guns and all.

You'll also want to visit the **Pemberton House** and the **Army Navy Museum**, located on Chestnut Street between 3rd and 4th. They have a large collection of army and navy war souvenirs, including cannons, flags, and uniforms. One

You have to sail 90 miles down the Delaware River to reach the Atlantic Ocean.

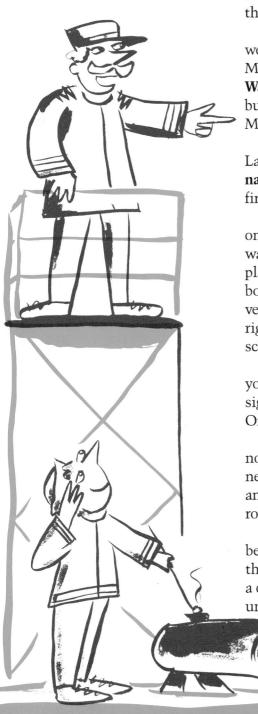

whole room is constructed to look and feel just like the deck of an old warship. You'll like the life-size figures and the 12-minute movie about the American Revolution.

And now that you've got your maritime feet wet, it's time to head east for the Delaware. The Maritime Museum runs a **Workshop on the Water** down on Penn's Landing where boat builders still work today. It's open from early May through mid-October.

But first, if you walk over the bridge to Penn's Landing, take a look at the Philadelphia **Vietnam Veterans Memorial** to your right. It's the first one in the country.

The Workshop on the Water is actually built on a floating barge that used to work the Delaware River. You have to cross over to it on a gangplank! Then once you get inside, watch how the boat builders make Tuck Ups, Duckers, and Garveys, some of the small crafts that were invented right in this region. Ask about their workshop schedule and see if you qualify to take a class.

If you're visiting during the summer months, you'll probably have to wait in line for a lot of the sights down at Penn's Landing. Try to be patient. Once you get in there, it'll be well worth it.

Now, just beyond the workshop, you probably noticed a ship and a submarine docked right next to each other. They are the USS *Olympia* and the USS *Becuna*. Both played important roles in America's naval history.

Board the *Olympia* first. Imagine it's November 5, 1892, and you've just signed on as part of this brand-new ship's seaworthy crew. You share a cabin with another sailor and stow your gear under your berth. Then you head for the kitchen where you're given a bushel of potatoes to peel.

Then imagine it's May 1, 1898, and you're facing the biggest challenge of your naval career. You're serving under Commodore Dewey in the Philippines and the Spanish fleet is about to blow you out of the water. But Dewey keeps his cool and seven long hours after he calmly gives the signal, "You may fire when you are ready, Gridley," all the Spanish ships are destroyed. Whew!

That'll give you some idea of what the *Olympia* has been through. It's the only ship that still exists from the Spanish-American War. Take a look at the huge black cannons that still stick out of their own portholes.

Visiting the USS *Becuna* is a whole different thing. This is a guppy-class submarine. Guppy? Yup, this submarine is very small. That is, small but highly effective. Toward the end of World War II, the *Becuna* searched out and destroyed many Japanese ships in the South Pacific.

You'll wonder how the sailors got along in such tight quarters. The passageways are narrow enough when you're a kid. Imagine a full-size adult male squeezing through them day after day. But the *Becuna* served the navy for twenty-five years, until 1969.

While you're navigating your way through the submarine, take a look at all the pressure valves and meters the sailors had to keep track of. Also, realize that while it's nice and still now, you can bet the *Becuna* sure rocked when it was out at sea.

If by now you're getting the itch to be cruising around the bay yourself, feeling the breeze in your hair, there are at least three different cruise lines you can choose from.

Near the bow of the USS **Olympia**, *you'll see a huge, framed American flag. It flew when the ship fought at the famous Battle of Manila Bay in 1898. The flag also covers up a big hole made by a cannon that slipped out of its hold. It crushed a seaman against the wall and some people say his ghost still haunts the ship. Ask a guide if anyone's heard Johnson roaming around lately!*

Schuylkill is easier to pronounce than it looks. Say **skoolkle!**

The ***Spirit of Philadelphia*** leaves from Penn's Landing at Spruce Street and offers full meals during your trip. **Liberty Belle Charters** leave from Pier 1 North at Race Street, and **R & S Harbor Tours** leave from Penn's Landing Marina at Lombard Street. Call ahead for departure times, and ask if you need to reserve a seat.

If it's May or June, head over to the Grand Plaza, where you might be able to catch the **Jambalaya Jam**. No, it's not another ship. It's a band of musicians who play New Orleans jazz, zydeco, Creole, and Dixieland music, straight out of Louisiana. This would be a golden opportunity to try Cajun food.

On the other side of the city, let's not forget the **Schuylkill River**. It was never wide enough to be a port so it has remained a place for Philadelphian parents and children to play on the weekend.

When the weather's nice, and even when it isn't, you can often see people out there rowing, canoeing, sculling, and doing crew. Many of them are part of a team that's either practicing for a race or actually racing. The crew teams are usually out there very early in the morning.

If you'd like to get out on the water, think about renting a canoe from the **Public Canoe House** on the Schuylkill. (The phone number is 225-3560.)

Or, if you would rather stay on dry land, rent a bicycle and ride along the many bike paths throughout Fairmount Park. Try **Fairmount Park Bike Rentals** on Kelly Drive at the Art Museum or the bike rental place at **One Boathouse Row**.

Do you like the zoo? Well, here is America's very first zoo, right in Philadelphia. The **Phila-**

delphia Zoo is located beyond the Museum of Art and covers 42 acres. It opened in 1874 and has many exhibits that take you very close to the animals. Like the Jungle Bird Walk where birds fly overhead, or the primate exhibit where you're only separated from lemurs and gorillas by moats.

In the Treehouse, you can crawl into a huge egg and imagine what it would feel like to hatch out of it or squeeze yourself through the cells of a honeycomb.

Later, in the Children's Zoo, take a pony ride or watch the sea lions swim right under your nose. That's also the only place in the zoo where you can actually help feed the animals.

In the Reptile House, snakes and tortoises get drenched in a simulated tropical thunderstorm throughout the day. And don't miss the African Plains exhibit where antelopes have plenty of room to leap and bound and run around next to the zebras and giraffes. You really get a good feeling for their natural habitat.

The zoo is located in the beautiful 200-year-old Fairmount Park. This park extends almost 9,000 acres, which makes it the largest landscaped city park in the world. And beginning in April, the dogwood and cherry blossoms turn it into a pink and flowery wonderland.

People go to the park to jog, ride a bike, have a picnic, play baseball, soccer, and tennis, swim in the summer, sled in the winter, ride horses, and just hang out.

The best way to get an overview of the park is to take the **Fairmount Park Trolley/Bus Tour**.

Then you can go back later to the places that interested you most during the tour.

The park is especially proud of its collection of handsome estates. Back in the 1700s and 1800s, the wealthy families of Philadelphia built them as country homes where they could get away on the weekends.

If you visit the **Japanese House**, you may be able to sit in on an ancient tea ceremony in progress. At the **Smith Civil War Monument**, you can sit on a famous "whispering bench."

The **Smith Memorial Playgrounds and Playhouse** have an awesome number of jungle gyms, swings, sliding boards, and other outdoor structures to play on.

For old doll and toy lovers, there's the **Strawberry House** and the **Woodford House**. And one of the best times of the year to visit these elegant homes is at Christmas time. They really get dressed up for holiday visitors.

9. Stockbrokers and Busybodies

While you're dodging pedestrians on Market Street, try to imagine this paved avenue with no cars and buses. Picture it as a dirt road filled with farmers and merchants hawking their food and wares from stalls covered with wooden sheds. Today, the faces and buildings may have changed, but it's still Philadelphia's liveliest place to do business.

If you've never seen stockbrokers and traders in action, a tour of the **Pennsylvania Stock Exchange** will give you some idea of what goes on behind the scenes with America's invested money. This Exchange is a minor player compared to New York and Chicago, but it's worth a visit.

Or, you can just watch from the windows downstairs in the building's atrium. The traders have to monitor the market constantly, with their eyes on a computer screen and their ears on the phone. They won't even notice you peering in!

David Rittenhouse was one of America's early astronomers and a good friend of Benjamin Franklin. He also gave his name to one of Philadelphia's chicest neighborhoods, **Rittenhouse**

Square. If you happen to like flowers and it's the month of May, head over to the Rittenhouse Square **Flower Market** for a sweet sniff. You'll be doing what Philadelphia families have been doing since 1914. The market also sells unusual snacks, like the mouth-watering lemon stick.

During the first two weeks of June, many artists from the Philadelphia area come and hang out their art on clotheslines at Rittenhouse. It's called the **Clothesline Art Exhibit**, and it's always packed with artists and buyers.

While famous people were putting their names on Philadelphia's parks, George Washington couldn't be overlooked. Today, our first president has got **Washington Square**, one of William Penn's original four squares designed for the city.

And this park is a full one. For example, the British and American soldiers who died of yellow fever are buried here right next to a handful of seeds that our astronauts brought to the moon and back. There's also the Tomb of the Unknown Soldier, which has an eternal flame. It's the only tomb in the United States put up to remind us of the unknown Revolutionary War soldier.

Speaking of that wise old man Ben Franklin again, let's take a look at another institution he helped set up back in 1755 in order to help his fellowman. It's the **Pennsylvania Hospital**, the oldest private hospital in the country.

It sure doesn't look like a hospital, with its red brick facade and pretty, homelike windows. On top of the main building, you'll see a white-domed rotunda. That was the surgical amphitheater where the doctors performed operations. They had to wait for high noon in order to have enough daylight.

*Curious about how many human beings now live on earth? Head around the corner from Ritten-house Park, on South 7th Street, and take a look in the window of the **U.S. Census Bureau**. They keep a computerized count of the world's popu-lation. At last count, it was well over five billion.*

And when you get up close, you'll see there's a sort of moat built around the hospital. That dates back to the time when the hospital was also an asylum for the mentally ill. Believe it or not, Philadelphians used to picnic on the hospital grounds and some of them made fun of the insane people who were getting their fresh air down in the moat!

If it's a hot day, take a break in the **Physic Garden**. In the hospital's early days, the staff needed a garden to grow medicinal herbs. You can find out how plants help cure our ailments. There's also a shaded walk for cooling off.

A few blocks east of the hospital, you'll be heading into **Society Hill**, a beautiful old neigh-borhood that really was a hill before the wear and tear of centuries finally flattened it out. You'll know you're there when the street lights have black stands and panels.

Plus, some of the houses have busybodies sticking out from the second floor. Ben Franklin saw these contraptions in Holland and brought them back to town. They're actually mirrors that point up and down the street. That way you can spy on your neighbors!

Also, watch for the boot scrapers near the stairways and the big brass knockers on the doors. They're reminders of the old days. And closer to Front Street, you'll find some quiet cobblestone streets, like old **Delancey Street**. You can practically see the old carriages riding along.

A few blocks southeast, you'll find **Head House Square** and its original brick shed. It still looks a lot like it did almost 200 years ago. Back then, farmers sold their butter and eggs on the west side, meat under the arcade, and herbs and vegetables on the east side. Fishmongers had to set up on the sidewalks. Guess why!

Today, the only people you'll find out there selling are the craftspeople. They set up special fairs every weekend evening during the summer.

Society Hill got its name from the group of businessmen and investors whom William Penn convinced to settle in Philadelphia in 1683. They called themselves the Free Society of Traders.

49

10. From Einstein to Zipperhead

Okay, so where do the Philadelphia kids go when they want a new game or a new hat or something funky to go with a new outfit? Here are a few of their favorite stores.

Let's start on **South Street**. The best part is between Front and 9th streets where you'll see street musicians, artists, European-style cafés, and lots of kids like you hanging out when the weather's warm.

A lot of the streets that shoot off South have some places to check out, too, so take a peek right and left when you're crossing them, especially Bainbridge.

To pick up some antique or unusual up-to-date clothing, try XOG, at 340 South, or Rope, at 514 South 4th. A few blocks down on South Street, drop in at The Last Wound-up, at number 617. They have old and new wind-up toys, including music boxes and stuffed animals. They're best known for Pudgey the Piglet and Wacko the Cockroach. You'll probably see the mechanical Pudgey wobbling around on the sidewalk out front, so try not to step on him!

If you're a hat maniac, you won't want to miss Hats in the Belfry, on the corner of South and

3rd. You can get something ordinary to put on your head or you can try a Viking helmet, horns and all. Then there's a three-cornered hat, if you're feeling very Napoleonic, or a top hat, if you're in the mood to get elegant.

And you won't be able to miss Zipperhead. That's the store with the giant black ants crawling all over the outside wall of the second story. Inside is just as funky. They've got long earrings, short dresses, pointed shoes, and an assortment of leather armbands. Get the picture?

If you're starting to get hungry for something sweet, grab a cookie at the Company Cookie, 418 South. They'll also scoop you some ice cream or throw together a bag of broken cookies. Broken cookies? It's cheaper that way and you get more variety.

Now, there are also some unique shops in other parts of the city and you can reach several of them on foot from South Street. One of the big mall-type hangouts for kids in Philadelphia is The Gallery I and Gallery II at Market Street East. At last count, there were more than 200 stores and restaurants spread out on four different floors.

It's right next to Strawbridge & Clothier, where the famous comedian W. C. Fields worked as a cash boy in 1893, when he was just 13. That was before there were child labor laws. His job was to run with cash all over the store, picking it up from cashiers and rushing it to the book-keepers. Today, if you're into trivia, you can buy a game called Philadelphia Trivia at Strawbridge or other stores.

Practically across the street from The Gallery is America's very first department store,

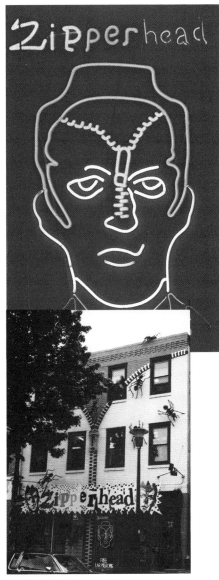

Philadelphians love antiques. Four blocks of Pine Street, from 9th to 12th, have over twenty-five antique shops. That's why they call Pine Street "antique row."

Wanamaker's. It takes up the whole city block between Market, Chestnut, 13th, and Juniper. Believe it or not, this big store starts the day with a bugle blowing at opening. And an enormous organ with 30,000 pipes gives a little daily concert at 11:15 and 5:15. Now, that's old-fashioned!

On the corner of Market and 7th, in the Mellon Independence Center, you'll find Einstein's Toys That Matter. These are definitely some of the most fun educational toys you'll ever see. Some of them were even invented by kids.

If you have one of those minds that's always trying to figure things out, you might want to see what The Compleat Strategist has to offer. It's at 2011 Walnut Street, and it's got everything you'd need for Dungeons & Dragons as well as many other great strategy games. So test your brains!

If you like doing and making things yourself, check out the How-to-do-it Bookstore, on 1608 Sansom. They have kits and books on just about anything you can think of.

By the way, Thomas Jefferson loved to shop. When you visit his rooms at the Graff House, you'll see stacks of shipping boxes. He had his favorite things sent over from Europe.

11. Flyers and Choirs

Philadelphia also has five college basketball teams. The team from Villanova won the 1985 NCAA championship.

If you're a big sports fan and want to cheer on some major players, Philadelphia's teams will give you lots of championship action. Philadelphia loves its sports teams live rather than on television, so it's a good idea to buy tickets as far in advance as possible. And if you like performances, including classical music and theater, Philadelphia's musicians and actors are also among the best.

From November through April, the **Philadelphia 76ers** professional basketball team heads off its opponents at the Spectrum, at Broad and Pattison streets. They play about forty games a season, and the 18,000 seats at the Spectrum are often sold out. And because the team is so good, they often go into the NBA playoffs in April.

While the 76ers are winding down their season in the spring, the **Philadelphia Phillies** are just getting warmed up. This pro baseball team plays day and night games at Veterans Stadium, also at Broad and Pattison, from April through October. The stadium can fit 64,000 fans, so you shouldn't have too much trouble getting tickets. And every time the Phillies play a home game on a Sunday, they give away free baseball caps and other paraphernalia.

Halfway through the Phillies' season, in August, the **Philadelphia Eagles** begin their season. Eagles tickets are harder to get than the 76ers and Phillies seats because Philadelphia is a real football town. The pro team is young but on the rise in the professional league. They also play at Veterans, through December, and even on the coldest days the stadium will be full of shivering fans. Call way ahead of time for these tickets.

And while Philadelphia loves football, basketball, and baseball, it probably loves hockey the best. You won't be able to hear or talk for days after a **Philadelphia Flyers** game at the Spectrum. And that's if you can find tickets at all. The

stadium is small, but the team's popularity is very big. So, while you're sitting home thinking about this trip, see about getting some Flyers tickets weeks or even months ahead of your arrival. Their season runs from October through April, too.

The Spectrum also hosts **rock concerts** throughout the year. Forget buying a ticket at the door; make sure you call a Ticketron outlet for a seat beforehand.

If you like classical music, be sure to visit the **Academy of Music**. You may have noticed it when you were walking around the city neighborhoods just south of Market Street. Six flickering original gaslights out front distinguish the academy at Broad and Locust streets, and it has some of the best acoustics in the country.

The **Walnut Street Theater** is the oldest American theater still in continuous use. It was founded in 1809 and presents five plays from November through April.

The academy is so popular that it offers a musical performance practically every night. You can also take a backstage tour and see what the performers' dressing rooms look like.

Boy students at the academy's Performing Arts School perform throughout the year as the **Academy Boys Choir**. The choir's 40 to 60 members are between seven and fifteen years old, and they sing everything from classical songs to Broadway tunes. If you like to sing, these beautiful concerts will really inspire you.

If you're in Philadelphia between Thanksgiving and Christmas, and you like ballet, watch the **Pennsylvania Ballet Company** dance Tchaikovsky's "The Nutcracker Suite" at the academy. Plus, the **Philadelphia Orchestra** gives a series of very fun children's concerts there. The Children's Concerts are short and full of easy explanations about the music and the instruments.

If you're thinking about a career in music some day, you might want to visit the **Curtis Institute of Music**, just off Rittenhouse Square. It's one of the top music schools in the country and has been teaching some of the most accomplished professional musicians for over sixty-five years. The institute gives free student recitals Monday, Wednesday, and Friday throughout the school year.

If you prefer theater, and you're in Philadelphia during the month of May, make sure to catch a performance at the **Annenberg Center Theatre for Children**. Their May festival, at 3680 Walnut Street, brings in an audience of kids from all over the state and beyond. The performers also come from all over the world to sing, dance, and mime just for you.

Want to get on television? Here are a few possibilities for you to arrange before you get to Philadelphia.

"Al Albert Showcase" is a talent show for kids that airs on Saturday mornings at 11:00 on WPVI-TV 6. Their auditions and tapings are from 7:00 to 10:00 p.m. on Wednesdays. Write to them at 4100 City Line Avenue, Philadelphia, PA 19104.

"Double Dare" is also taped in Philadelphia. You have to write beforehand if you want to audition or be a member of the studio audience. The address: Double Dare, 1775 Broadway, New York, NY 10019. (Yep, that's a New York address even though the show is produced in Philly.)

12. Getting Out of Town: Battlefields and Gardens

W hile Philadelphia was growing and carving out its identity, the areas surrounding it were hardly standing still. There are many counties to visit, each with its own distinctive character. Also, the environs of Philadelphia boast a number of historical events that helped shape the nation.

Southwest of Philadelphia, you'll be entering Chester County and Brandywine Valley. Children and adults love to visit the 350 world-famous acres of **Longwood Gardens**. It's open every day. Besides some of the most gorgeous flowerbeds in the country, they offer music, art, theater, and Fourth of July fireworks.

The **Valley Forge National Historic Park** is also in Chester County, west of Philadelphia. Imagine it's the long, bitter winter of 1777 and you're one of George Washington's troops. Check out the reproduced soldiers' huts and Washington's actual headquarters. Those soldiers and their leaders were really dedicated to the cause.

North of the city, you'll be heading into **Bucks County**, which is west of the Delaware River. This is where General Washington made his famous crossing of the Delaware, and there's even a town called Washington Crossing.

While the British occupied Philadelphia, during the winter of 1777-78, 12,000 American soldiers in the Continental Army camped at Valley Forge under General George Washington. It was so cold that almost 2,000 men and boys died. But by spring, they were ready to fight again.

Bucks County also claims a large number of craftspeople who have many shops and galleries throughout the area. **Sesame Place** in Langhorne has amusement rides and attractions with Bert, Ernie, and the rest of the Sesame Street gang. Bring a bathing suit because Sesame Place also has a fantastic set of water games.

Farther west of Philadelphia, you'll find Pennsylvania's famous **Lancaster County**, known for its Amish, or Pennsylvania Dutch, residents. They watch no television or videos and often have no electricity in their homes. And it's not because they're poor. They just prefer a simple, quiet life.

Most Amish are farmers and cultivate the same fertile fields their ancestors plowed hundreds of years ago. They don't drive cars, either. Instead, you'll see them trotting along in their black horse-drawn carriages, sometimes on the way to a one-room schoolhouse where the children have their lessons.

They often dress in black, with the women and girls in long dresses and bonnets. The men and boys also wear distinctive hats and everyone speaks the Amish dialect. There are many museums, markets, and special houses to visit in Lancaster County, all to give you a feel for how these proud people live.

Details

Academy of Music
Broad and Locust Streets
Philadelphia, PA 19103
(215) 222-2101

Academy of Natural Sciences
19th Street and the Parkway
Philadelphia, PA 19103
(215) 299-1000
Handicapped Access

Afro-American Historical and Cultural Museum
7th and Arch Streets
Philadelphia, PA 19106
(215) 574-0380
Handicapped Access

American Swedish Historical Museum
1900 Pattison Avenue
Philadelphia, PA 19145
(215) 389-1776

Annenberg Center Theatre for Children
3680 Walnut Street
Philadelphia, PA 19103
(215) 898-6791

Atwater Kent Museum
15 South 7th Street
Philadelphia, PA 19106
(215) 686-3630, or 922-3031
Handicapped Access

Balch Institute for Ethnic Studies
18 South 7th Street
Philadelphia, PA 19106
(215) 925-8090
Handicapped Access

Betsy Ross House
239 Arch Street
Philadelphia, PA 19107
(215) 627-5343

Christ Church
2nd and Market Streets
Philadelphia, PA 19106
(215) 922-1695

Fairmount Park Trolley Tours
(215) 636-1666

Fireman's Hall Museum
Second and Quarry Streets
Philadelphia, PA 19106
(215) 922-9844
Handicapped Access

Franklin Court
314-322 Market Street
Philadelphia, PA 19106
(215) 597-2760
Handicapped Access

Franklin Institute Science Museum and Fels Planetarium
20th Street and Ben Franklin Parkway
Philadelphia, PA 19103
(215) 564-3375 recorded, or 448-1200
Handicapped Access

Free Library of Philadelphia
Logan Square
Philadelphia, PA 19103
(215) 686-5372

Historical Society of Pennsylvania
1300 Locust Street
Philadelphia, PA 19107
(215) 732-6200
Handicapped Access

Independence Hall
Chestnut Street between 5th and 6th Streets
Philadelphia, PA 19106
(215) 627-1776 recorded, or 597-7081
Limited Handicapped Access

Independence National Historical Park Visitor Center
3rd Street between Chestnut and Walnut Streets
Philadelphia, PA 19106
(215) 597-8974

Lancaster County, Pennsylvania Dutch Visitors Bureau
501 Greenfield Road
Lancaster, PA 17601
(717) 299-8901

Liberty Bell Charters, Inc.
Pier 1 North, Delaware River at Race Street
Philadelphia, PA 19106
(215) 238-0887

Liberty Bell Pavilion
Independence Mall, Market Street between
5th and 6th Streets
Philadelphia, PA 19106
(215) 627-1776 recorded, or 597-2458
Handicapped Access

Longwood Gardens
Route 1, Box 501
Kennett Square, PA 19348-0501
(215) 388-6741
Handicapped Access

Mummers Museum
2nd and Washington Avenue
Philadelphia, PA 19147
(215) 336-3050
Handicapped Access

National Museum of American Jewish History
Independence Mall East, 55 North 5th Street
Philadelphia, PA 19106
(215) 923-3811
Limited Handicapped Access

Pemberton House
(Army Navy Museum)
Chestnut Street between 3rd and 4th Streets
Philadelphia, PA 19106
(215) 627-1776 recorded, or 597-2458
Limited Handicapped Access

Pennsylvania Hospital and Nursing Museum
8th and Spruce Streets
Philadelphia, PA 19107
(215) 829-3971
Handicapped Access

Philadelphia Maritime Museum
321 Chestnut Street
Philadelphia, PA 19106
(215) 925-5439

Philadelphia Maritime Museum's Workshop on the Water
Boat Basin at Penn's Landing
Philadelphia, PA 19106
(215) 925-7589
Handicapped Access

Philadelphia Museum of Art
26th Street and Ben Franklin Parkway
P.O. Box 7646
Philadelphia, PA 19101
(215) 763-8100, or 787-5488 for daily events
Handicapped Access

Philadelphia Zoo
34th Street and Girard Avenue
Philadelphia, PA 19104
(215) 243-1100
Handicapped Access

Please Touch Museum
210 North 21st Street
Philadelphia, PA 19103
(215) 963-0666, or 963-0667 for current activities
Handicapped Access

Public Canoe House
Schuylkill River
(215) 225-3560

R & S Harbor Tours, Inc.
Penn's Landing Marina
Delaware River at Lombard Street
Philadelphia, PA 19106
(215) 928-0972

Sesame Place
Oxford Valley Road
Langhorne, PA 19407
(215) 757-1100 recorded, or 752-7070
Handicapped Access

Spirit of Philadelphia
Penn's Landing Marina
Delaware River at Spruce Street
Philadelphia, PA 19106
(215) 923-4962, or 923-4993

University Museum of Archaeology and Anthropology
University of Pennsylvania
33rd and Spruce Streets
Philadelphia, PA 19104
(215) 898-4000, or 222-7777
for current events
Handicapped Access

USS *Becuna*, USS *Olympia*
Delaware River waterfront, between
Market and Lombard
Philadelphia, PA 19106
(215) 922-1898

Valley Forge National Historic Park
Valley Forge, PA 19481-0953
(215) 783-1077
Handicapped Access

Washington Crossing Historic Park
Washington Crossing, PA 18977
(215) 493-4076
Handicapped Access

Kidding Around with John Muir Publications

We are making the world more accessible for young travelers. In your hand you have one of several John Muir Publications guides written and designed especially for kids. We will be *Kidding Around* other cities also. Send us your thoughts, corrections, and suggestions. We also publish other books about travel and other subjects. Let us know if you would like one of our catalogs.

TITLES NOW
AVAILABLE IN THE
SERIES

Kidding Around Atlanta
Kidding Around Boston
Kidding Around Chicago
Kidding Around the Hawaiian Islands
Kidding Around London
Kidding Around Los Angeles
Kidding Around the National Parks
   of the Southwest
Kidding Around New York City
Kidding Around Philadelphia
Kidding Around San Francisco
Kidding Around Washington, D.C.

John Muir Publications
P.O. Box 613
Santa Fe, New Mexico 87504
(505) 982-4078